what NOT to name your

baby

by Andy Meisler
and Michael Rey

Ten Speed Press
Berkeley, California

A Kirsty Melville book

 Ten Speed Press
P.O. Box 7123
Berkeley, CA 94707

Distributed in Australia by E.J. Dwyer Pty Ltd;
in Canada by Publishers Group West; in
New Zealand by Tandem Press; in South Africa
by Real Books; and in the United Kingdom
and Europe by Airlift Books.

Art direction and design by Rey international, LA
Printed in Hong Kong

Library of Congress
Cataloging-in-Publication Data

Meisler, Andy.
What not to name your baby
by Andy Meisler and Michael Rey.
p. cm.   ISBN 0-89815-814-1
1. Names, Personal–Dictionaries.
I. Rey, Michael.   II. Title.
CS2377.M45   1996
929.4 4–dc20
95-39813

3 4 5 6 7 8 9 10 – 99 98 97 96

To the millions yet unnamed:

Adolf

Alf

Aloysius

Amadeus

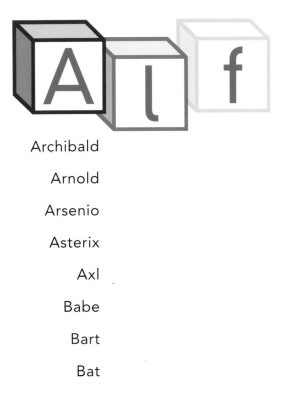

Archibald

Arnold

Arsenio

Asterix

Axl

Babe

Bart

Bat

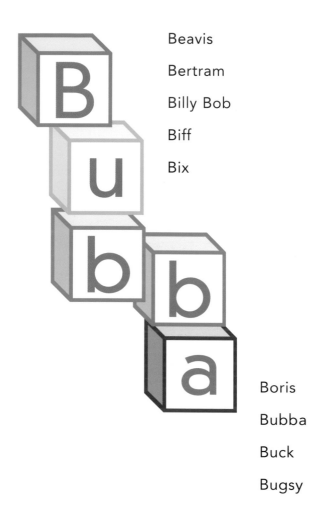

Beavis

Bertram

Billy Bob

Biff

Bix

Boris

Bubba

Buck

Bugsy

Buster

Bruce Lee

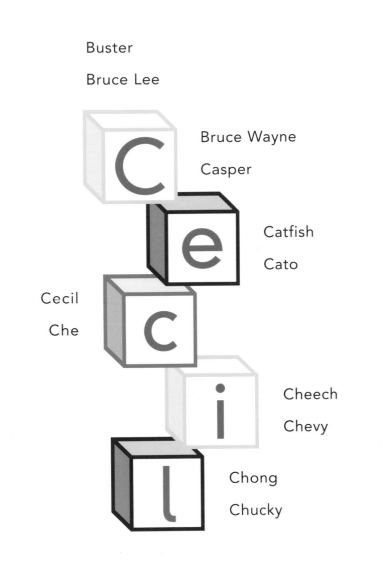

Bruce Wayne

Casper

Catfish

Cato

Cecil

Che

Cheech

Chevy

Chong

Chucky

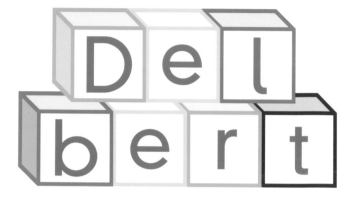

Cosmo

Curly

Dagwood   Dilbert

Cisco   Delbert   Dinty

Clem   Dobie

Clyde   Egbert

Conan

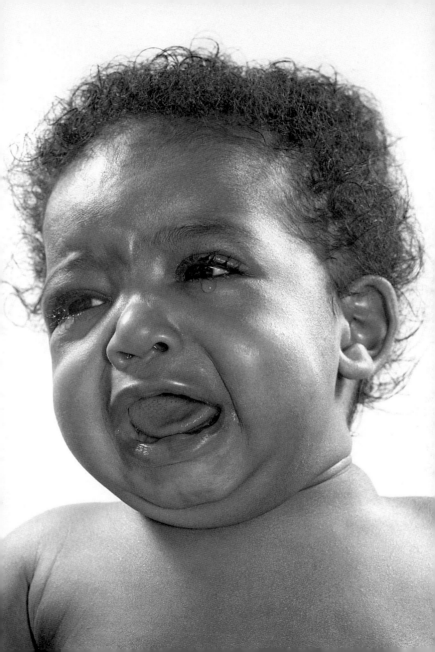

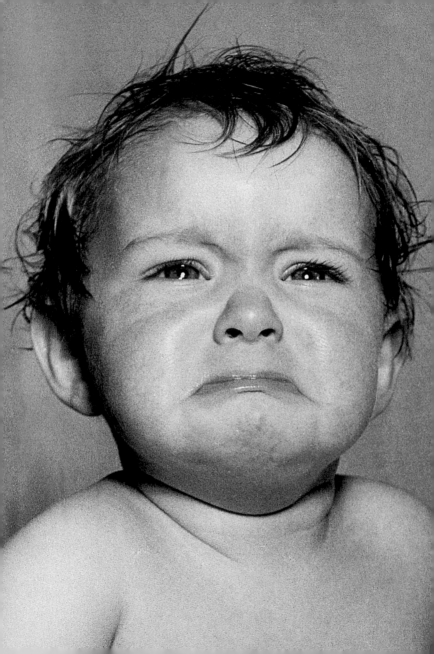

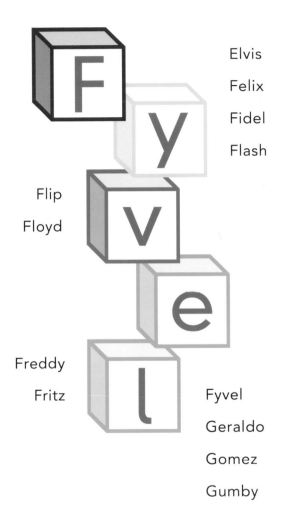

Elvis
Felix
Fidel
Flash

Flip
Floyd

Freddy
Fritz

Fyvel
Geraldo
Gomez
Gumby

Hamlet

Hawk

Hekyll

Herbert

Hercules

Herman

Homer

Horace

Howdy

Hulk

Humbert

Idi

Ignatz

Indiana   Ishmael

Irving   Izzy

        Jack Daniel

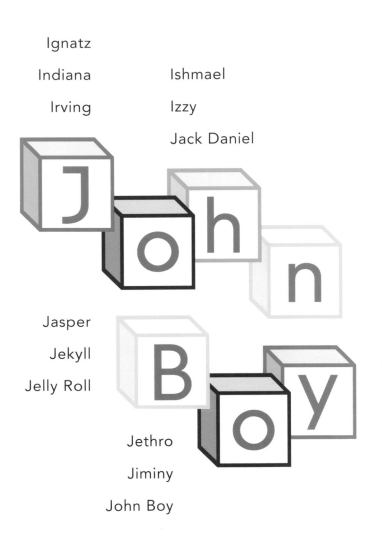

Jasper

Jekyll

Jelly Roll

        Jethro

        Jiminy

        John Boy

Jor-el

J. Edgar

J.R.

Kato   Lancelot

Kermit   Latka

Kukla   Lefty

Louie

Lucky

Mao

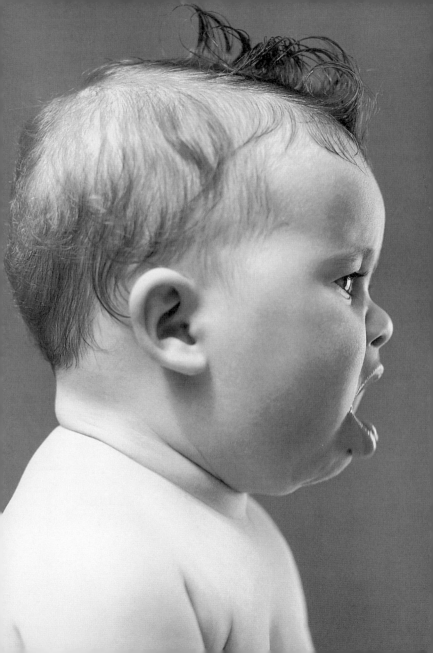

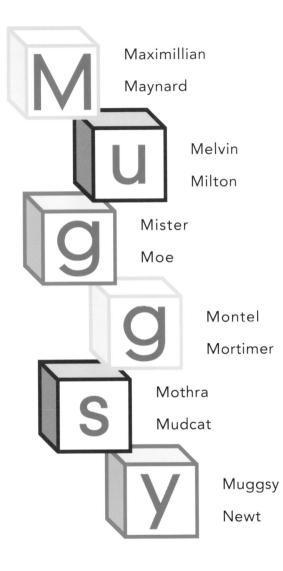

Maximillian

Maynard

Melvin

Milton

Mister

Moe

Montel

Mortimer

Mothra

Mudcat

Muggsy

Newt

Nitro

Nostradamus

Oedipus

Ollie

Onan

Opie

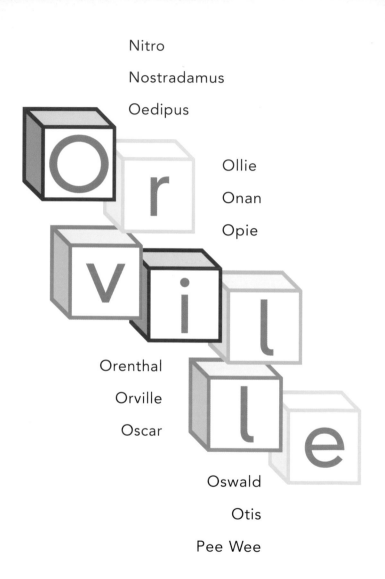

Orenthal

Orville

Oscar

Oswald

Otis

Pee Wee

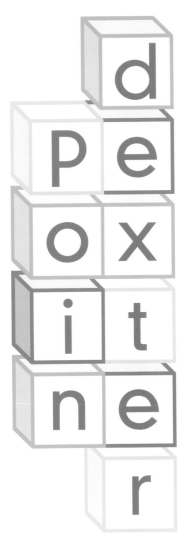

Peg Leg

Philbert

Philo   Quentin

Pinocchio   Quincy

Poindexter   Rambo

♀   Ramtha

Puck

Pudd'nhead

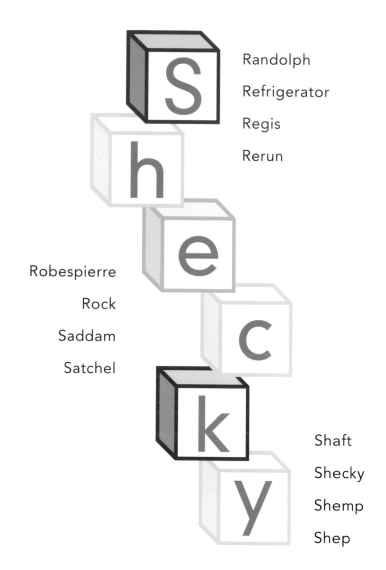

Randolph
Refrigerator
Regis
Rerun

Robespierre
Rock
Saddam
Satchel

Shaft
Shecky
Shemp
Shep

Skeets

Sherlock Skeezix Snuffy

Shorty Slappy Sluggo Soapy

Sigmund Sly Sol

Snoop

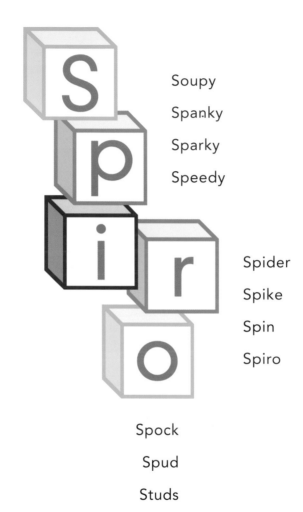

Soupy

Spanky

Sparky

Speedy

Spider

Spike

Spin

Spiro

Spock

Spud

Studs

Sue

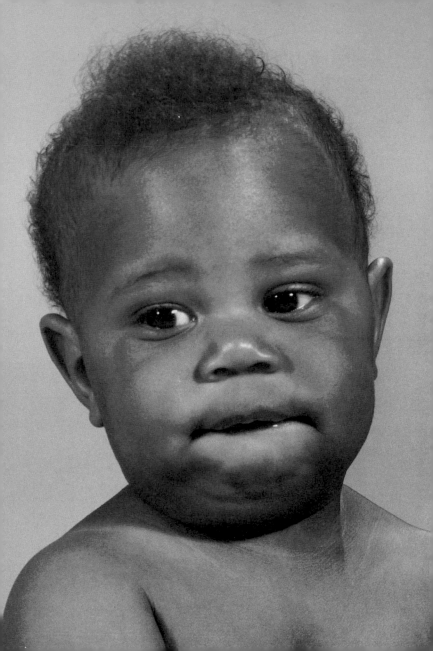

Sylvester

Swifty

Tab

T-Bone

Tennessee

Tito

Titus

Turbo

Virgil

Wendell

Whizzer

Wilbur

Wilmer

Wink

Winston

Wolfgang

Virgil   Yo Yo

Virgo   Yugo

Yankel   Zippy

Yentl   Zooey

            Zorro

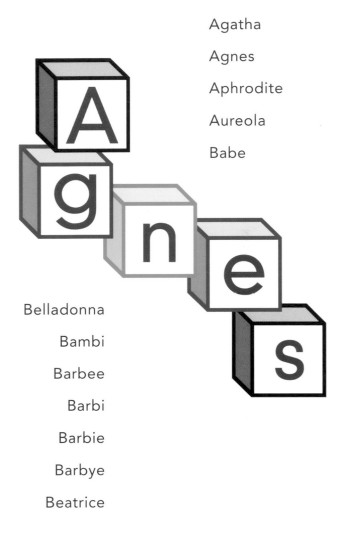

Agatha

Agnes

Aphrodite

Aureola

Babe

Belladonna

Bambi

Barbee

Barbi

Barbie

Barbye

Beatrice

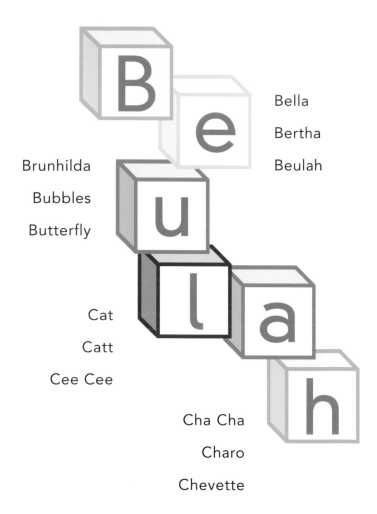

Bella
Bertha
Beulah

Brunhilda
Bubbles
Butterfly

Cat
Catt
Cee Cee

Cha Cha
Charo
Chevette

Cinderella

Clarabelle

Cleopatra

Clytemnestra

Cookie

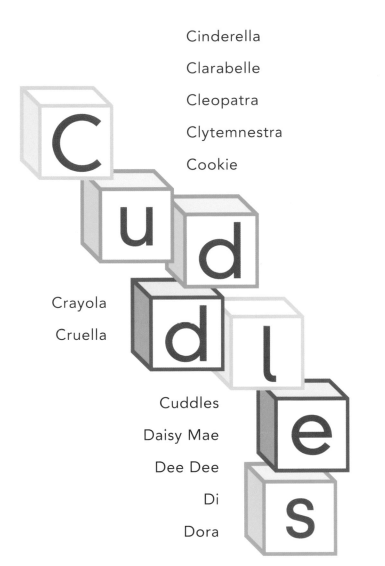

Crayola

Cruella

Cuddles

Daisy Mae

Dee Dee

Di

Dora

Dottie

Edna

Edwina

Effie

Elly May

Fergie

Fifi

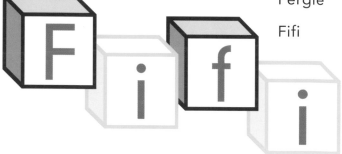

Endora

Enola

Ethel

Ethyl

Fannie Mae

Flo

Flossie

Frankie

Fresca

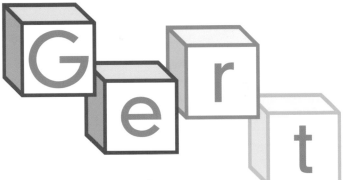

Gee Gee

Gennifer

Gert

Gertie

Gertrude

Gidget

Gigi

Ginger

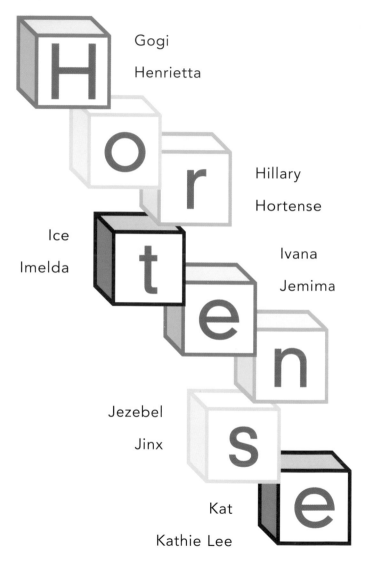

Gogi

Henrietta

Hillary

Hortense

Ice

Imelda

Ivana

Jemima

Jezebel

Jinx

Kat

Kathie Lee

Kennedy

Lassie

La Toya

Laverne

Leia

Leona

Lisa Marie

Lizzie

Lulu

Lycra

Madge

Madonna

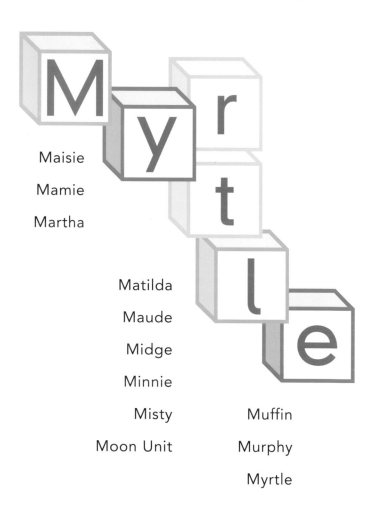

Maisie

Mamie

Martha

Matilda

Maude

Midge

Minnie

Misty   Muffin

Moon Unit   Murphy

               Myrtle

Natasha

Ophelia

Oprah

Pansy

Patsy

Peaches

Pebbles

Pepsi

Pickles

Pippi

Pocahontas

Pollyanna

Prunella

Polly Esther   Queenie   Saffron

Precious   Rapunzel   Sally Jesse

Princess   Rolanda   Salmonella

Roseanne

Rotunda

Selma

Sinsemilla

Siren

Soon Yi

Swoozie

Thelma

Tillie

Tinkerbelle

Tipper

Tondalayo

Trixie

Tuesday

Twiggy

Vanity   Venus De Milo

Velma   Velveeta

Vendela

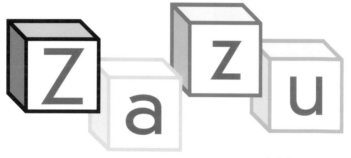

Zelda

Wednesday   Zinnia

Wilhelmina   Zsa Zsa

Wilma

Zasu

SAVE THE CHILDREN

We are currently compiling names
and (non-returnable) photographs
for future editions of this book.
Please send your suggestions to:

WNTNYB
Suite M-108
11802 Washington Boulevard
Los Angeles, CA 90066

Fax: 310-551-1732
e-mail: mbmx50a@prodigy.com